W9-ACF-601

Famous Explorers™

Hernán Cortés

Jeff
Donaldson-Forbes

The Rosen Publishing Group's
PowerKids Press™
New York

To Jacob and Eli Cytrynbaum

Published in 2002 by The Rosen Publishing Group, Inc.
29 East 21st Street, New York, NY 10010

First Edition

Book Design: Maria E. Melendez and Felicity Erwin
Project Editor: Kathy Campbell

Photo Credits: Cover and title page © SuperStock; pp. 4 (Cortés), 4 (University of Salamanca), 6, 7 (map), 7 (ships), 8 (inset), 10, 11 (bottom), 12 (top), 15, 16 (bottom, left), 18 © North Wind Pictures; pp. 8, 11 (top), 12, (bottom), 16 (bottom, right), 19 (top), 19 (bottom) © The Granger Collection, New York; p 16 (mask) © Charles & Josette Lenars/CORBIS; p. 20 (bottom) © Maps.com/CORBIS; p. 20 (bottom) Gianni Dagli Orli/CORBIS.

Donaldson-Forbes, Jeff.
   Hernán Cortés / Jeff Donaldson-Forbes. — 1st ed.
      p. cm. — (Famous explorers)
   ISBN 0-8239-5832-9
   1. Cortés, Hernán, 1485–1547—Juvenile literature. 2. Mexico—History—Conquest, 1519-15-40—Juvenile literature. 3. Mexico—Discovery and exploration—Spanish—Juvenile literature. 4. Conquerors—Mexico—Biography—Juvenile literature. 5. Explorers—Mexico—Biography—Juvenile literature. 6. Explorers—Spain—Biography—Juvenile literature. I. Title. II. Series.

F1230.C835 D66 2002
972'.02—dc21
                                                                    00-011842

Manufactured in the United States of America

Contents

4

A Student of the Law

Hernán Cortés was born in 1485 in Medellín, Spain. His father was a captain in the Spanish army. Cortés's parents did not want their son to become a soldier like his father. They wanted him to get a good education and to become a lawyer. Cortés studied at the University of Salamanca and was a good student. His heart was not in his studies, though. He had heard stories of Spaniards searching for new ocean routes to Asia. He wanted to join these great **explorers**. After studying for two years, Cortés returned to Medellín in 1501. His parents were disappointed that he had not become a lawyer. Although he tried to find a job that would satisfy them, he could not find one. They agreed to pay for him to travel to the island of Hispaniola in the Caribbean Sea. Cortés's father had a friend there, and he hoped the friend would put Cortés to work.

Left: *Hernán Cortés wanted to become an explorer, although his parents wanted him to be a lawyer.* Right: *This gateway is at the University of Salamanca in Spain, where Cortés studied law for two years.*

Life on Hispaniola

Ovando was the governor of Hispaniola.

The island of Hispaniola (known today as Haiti and the Dominican Republic) was the capital of the Spanish **territories** in the Caribbean Sea during the late 1400s. In the early 1500s, Hispaniola was used as a base for Spanish **expeditions** to Mexico, Panama, and South America. Cortés sailed from Spain to Hispaniola in 1504. The ship's mast was damaged in a storm. When he arrived, Cortés went to Ovando, the **governor** of Hispaniola and an old friend of Cortés's father. Ovando granted Cortés a piece of land for farming and some native **slaves** to work for him. The Spaniards forced natives into slavery. The slaves did not give up their freedom willingly, and there were **violent** uprisings.

Top: A map from 1556 shows "Isola Spagnuola," or Island of Hispaniola. During Cortés's trip to Hispaniola, the ship became lost in a storm. It was said that a dove helped lead the ship to Hispaniola. Bottom: Cortés sailed to Hispaniola in a ship like one of these.

TRAMONTANA
ISOLA SPAGNVOLA
TORTVGA
NATIVITA
ISABELLA VECCHIA
P. PLATA
P. S. NICOLO
C. CABRON
XAMANA
CAIABO
GVANABA
PONENTE
LEVANTE
GVACAYARIMA
C. TIBVRON
S. DOMINICO
C. HIGVEY
MONA
SAONA
S. GIOVANNI
C. DE LOBOS
BEATA

Velázquez and Cuba

While living in Hispaniola, Cortés got to know an important man. Diego Velázquez was a **lieutenant governor**. Velázquez planned to sail to the island of Cuba and establish a new Spanish colony there. Cortés joined Velázquez's expedition. They arrived in Cuba in 1511. They claimed Cuba in the name of King Ferdinand of Spain. Velázquez became governor of Cuba. Soon Cortés was running a successful farm. He forced the natives to become slaves. They tilled the land, raised sheep and cattle, and mined for gold. Cortés became rich and powerful. Velázquez feared that Cortés might try to become governor. He arrested Cortés for plotting against him, but later set him free.

Top: Diego Velázquez, as Cuba's governor, divided the land of Cuba among the Spaniards. He and the other Spaniards made slaves of the natives. Bottom: Cortés and a native leader oversee slaves in building boats.

Gold from Yucatán

In 1519, Cortés led a voyage to Yucatán, Mexico.

In 1517, a Spanish expedition returned to Cuba from the Yucatán **peninsula** in eastern Mexico. The soldiers brought back gold objects they had stolen from Native American temples in Yucatán. Velázquez sent two more expeditions to Mexico over the next two years, hoping to discover more gold. The expeditions did not return when they were supposed to. Cortés believed they might never come back. He got permission from Velázquez to go to Mexico to find gold and claim new territories for Spain. Cortés used his own money to hire soldiers and sailors. In February 1519, Cortés sailed from Cuba with 11 ships and about 600 men. He sailed first to the island of Cozumel, off the eastern coast of Yucatán.

Top: Cortés watches the building of ships for his expedition into Mexico. Bottom: This map shows the places Cortés traveled during his trip from Cuba to Yucatán to Mexico.

Different Gods

When Cortés and his men arrived in Cozumel, he ordered them to treat the Native Americans with respect. He presented their leaders with gifts, including glass beads and steel knives. He met a Spanish priest, Jerónimo de Aguilar, who had been captured by the Native Americans on an earlier expedition. Cortés traded beads for the priest's freedom and Aguilar became Cortés's **interpreter**.

Like many European explorers, Cortés believed that all Native Americans must be **converted** to the Christian religion to save their souls. Cortés ordered them to stop worshiping their own gods. He told them that they should worship the Christian god instead. When they refused, Cortés's men destroyed the Native Americans' statues. Then, on March 4, 1519, Cortés left Cozumel and sailed to Yucatán.

Top: Cortés told the Native Americans they had to worship the Christian god. When they refused, Cortés's men destroyed the natives' religious statues. Bottom: This picture from 1612 shows a priest teaching the Native Americans in Mexico about the Christian religion.

13

The Battle of Tabasco

In Yucatán, Aguilar traveled ahead of Cortés's men to greet Native Americans in a town called Tabasco. The Tabascans did not trust the Spaniards because they had fought with men from the earlier Cuban expeditions. The Tabascans told Aguilar that they would not cooperate with Cortés. Cortés decided he must change his approach to get what he wanted. He ordered his men to attack Tabasco. On March 25, 1519, Cortés's men attacked the Tabascans with guns, cannons, steel spears, and horses. The Tabascans fought with clubs and other **primitive** weapons. They were terrified of the Spanish cannons and horses. They believed that a horse and its rider were one creature with two heads. Cortés's men defeated the Tabascans and killed thousands. They took control of the town. Cortés ordered the **survivors** to bring all their gold to him.

In the Battle of Tabasco, many Tabascans stopped fighting and ran away from the Spaniards in fear. They had never seen horses before, and they were afraid of the cannons. Cortés ordered the Tabascans who survived to bring all their gold to him.

Aztec Gold

Cortés was angry that the Tabascans did not bring him much gold. They told him about the Aztec Empire farther west in Mexico. Soon Cortés and his men sailed west. Friendly Native Americans greeted them in a town known today as Veracruz. They told Cortés about Montezuma, who ruled the Aztec Empire from the capital city of Tenochtitlán (pronounced tay-noch-teet-LAHN). Cortés told them that he had come as a friend and would like to meet Montezuma. Montezuma sent gifts of gold and silver, but he refused to meet Cortés. He believed that Cortés was the white-skinned Aztec god, Quetzalcoatl (pronounced kwet-sel-keh-WAH-tul). According to a religious story, this god would destroy Montezuma. Montezuma's gifts made Cortés certain that Tenochtitlán was the source of more gold.

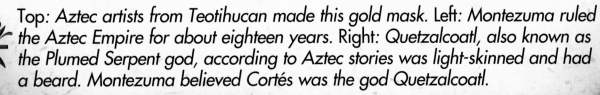

Top: Aztec artists from Teotihucan made this gold mask. Left: Montezuma ruled the Aztec Empire for about eighteen years. Right: Quetzalcoatl, also known as the Plumed Serpent god, according to Aztec stories was light-skinned and had a beard. Montezuma believed Cortés was the god Quetzalcoatl.

The Battle of Tlaxcala

Cortés led the expedition west, toward Tenochtitlán. In August 1519, they came to the city of Tlaxcala (pronounced tlah-SKA-lah) in central Mexico. The Tlaxcalans were enemies of the Aztecs. They had heard about Montezuma's gifts to Cortés, and believed the Spanish soldiers were **allies** of the Aztecs. On September 5, 1519, six thousand Tlaxcalans attacked Cortés's expedition. The Spaniards fought hard and killed women and children. Finally the Tlaxcalan chiefs decided to make peace. They were afraid the Spaniards would destroy their city. On September 18, 1519, they made peace with Cortés and his men. The Tlaxcalans joined forces with Cortés to **conquer** Tenochtitlán.

The Spaniards brought horses to Mexico.

Top: *An Aztec drawing shows the Tlaxcalans marching with Cortés's men to attack Tenochtitlán. Bottom: This Aztec drawing shows the Spaniards and the Tlaxcalans fighting with other Native Americans.*

guzmã. michvacã.

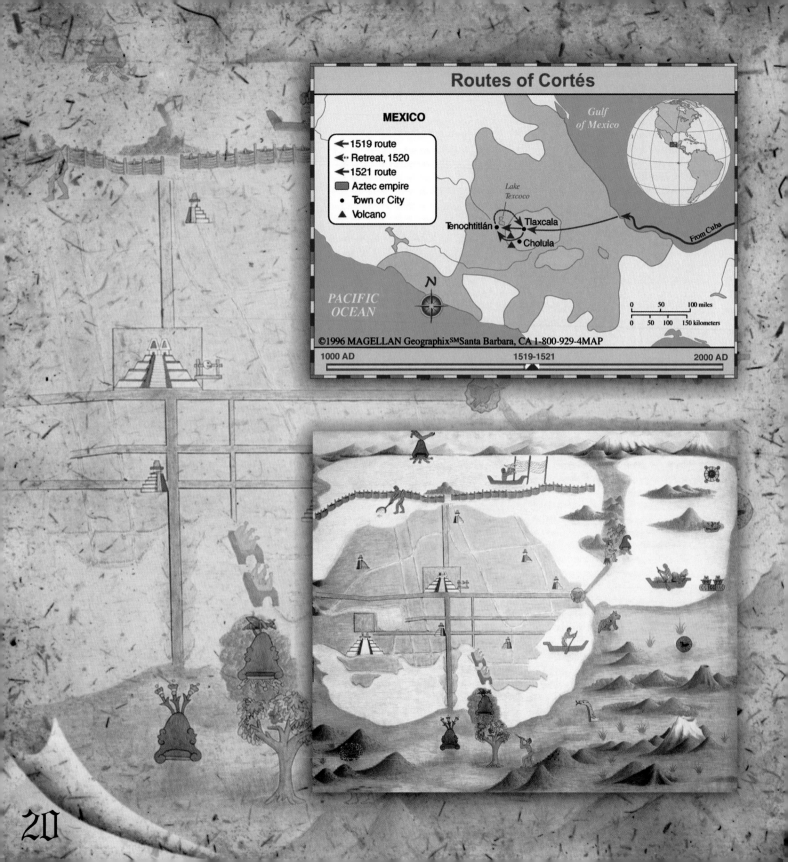

Routes of Cortés

MEXICO

1519 route
Retreat, 1520
1521 route
Aztec empire
• Town or City
▲ Volcano

Gulf of Mexico

Lake Texcoco

Tenochtitlán • Tlaxcala
▲ • Cholula

From Cuba

PACIFIC OCEAN

N

0   50   100 miles
0   50 100 150 kilometers

©1996 MAGELLAN Geographix℠ Santa Barbara, CA 1-800-929-4MAP

1000 AD   1519-1521   2000 AD

Tenochtitlán

This is a model of the Great Temple in Tenochtitlán.

On November 8, 1519, Cortés led his army of Spanish soldiers and Tlaxcalan warriors into Tenochtitlán. At its center stood the Great Temple, an enormous, stepped **pyramid**. At last the Spanish explorer came face to face with Montezuma. They presented each other with gifts. Cortés knew that Montezuma believed him to be the Aztec god Quetzalcoatl. He pretended to be this god to frighten Montezuma. Montezuma ordered the Aztec people to treat Cortés and his army with respect. Cortés did not plan to leave Tenochtitlán without claiming the city for Spain. Cortés was forced to change his plans, though. His former friend, Velázquez, had sent soldiers to Veracruz to arrest Cortés.

Top: This map shows the 1519, 1520, and 1521 routes followed into Mexico by Cortés and his men. Bottom: This picture of Tenochtitlán is from an ancient Aztec book. Tenochtitlán, the capital of the Aztec Empire, was founded in 1325, on an island. It was protected against floods by dams.

21

An Empire Destroyed

Cortés conquered Velázquez in Veracruz and returned to Tenochtitlán. The Aztecs had plotted to attack the Spanish army. Cortés captured Montezuma and used him to control the Aztecs. When Montezuma tried to talk to them, he was stoned to death by the Aztecs. Many Spaniards were killed as they retreated to Tlaxcala. In May 1521, Cortés attacked Tenochtitlán, and this time, he succeeded. The Aztec Empire fell on August 13. Cortés ruled Mexico until 1528. He found the gold he searched for, but he got it by killing thousands and by destroying the Aztec Empire. Hernán Cortés returned to Spain and died there on December 2, 1547.

Cortés's Timeline

1485	Hernán Cortés is born in Medellín, Spain.
1504	Cortés sails from Spain to Hispaniola.
1511	Cortés sails with Velázquez's expedition to settle Cuba.
1519	Cortés's expedition attacks Tabasco. Cortés leads an expedition to Tenochtitlán.
1521	Cortés destroys Tenochtitlán. The Aztec Empire falls on August 13.
1547	Cortés dies in Spain on December 2.

Glossary

allies (A-lyz) Groups of people that agree to help another group of people.

conquer (KON-ker) To overcome or get the better of something.

converted (kuhn-VER-tid) Change to a different religious belief.

expeditions (ek-spuh-DIH-shunz) Trips made for a special purpose, such as scientific study.

explorers (ik-SPLOR-urz) People who travel to different places to learn more about them.

governor (GUH-vuh-nur) An official who is put in charge of a colony by a king or queen.

interpreter (in-TER-preh-ter) A person who explains orally the meaning of one language and changes, or translates, it into another.

lieutenant governor (loo-TEH-nent GUH-vun-er) An official who ranks one step below a governor, and serves as the governor's second in command.

peninsula (peh-NIN-suh-luh) A piece of land that sticks into water from a larger body of land.

primitive (PRIH-muh-tiv) Something that has to do with an early stage of development.

pyramid (PEER-uh-mid) A large, stone structure with a square bottom and triangular sides that meet at a point on top.

slaves (SLAYVS) People who are owned by someone.

survivors (sur-VY-vurz) People who have stayed alive.

territories (TEHR-uh-tohr-eez) Lands that are controlled by a person or a group of people.

violent (VY-oh-lent) Strong, rough force.

Index

Web Sites

To learn more about Hernán Cortés, check out these Web sites:
www.acs.ucalgary.ca/HIST/tutor/eurvoya/aztec.html
www.encyclopedia.com/articles/03174.html